Lifelines

Edexcel GCSE Music

by

Julia Winterson

R·

Rhinegold Publishing Limited
241 Shaftesbury Avenue
London
WC2H 8TF
Telephone: 020 7333 1720
Fax: 020 7333 1765
www.rhinegold.co.uk

Rhinegold Music Study Guides
(series editor: Paul Terry)

Students' Guides to GCSE, AS and A2 Music for the AQA, Edexcel and OCR Specifications
Listening Tests for GCSE, AS and A2 Music for the AQA, Edexcel and OCR Specifications

A Student's Guide to GCSE Music for the WJEC Specification
A Student's Guide to Music Technology for the Edexcel AS and A2 Specification
Listening Tests for Students: Edexcel AS and A2 Music Technology Specification

The following books are designed to prepare for and support all GCSE and A-level music courses:
Key Stage 3 Listening Tests: Book 1
Music Literacy Workbook (for GCSE and A-level)
A Student's Guide to Harmony and Counterpoint (for AS and A2 Music)

Other Rhinegold Study Guides
A Student's Guide to AS Classical Civilisation for the AQA Specification
Students' Guides to AS and A2 Drama and Theatre Studies for the AQA and Edexcel Specifications
Students' Guides to AS and A2 Performance Studies for the OCR Specification
Students' Guides to AS and A2 Religious Studies for the AQA, Edexcel and OCR Specifications

Rhinegold Publishing also publishes Classical Music, Classroom Music, Early Music Today, Music Teacher,
Opera Now, Piano, The Singer, Teaching Drama, British and International Music Yearbook, British Performing
Arts Yearbook, Music Education Yearbook, Rhinegold Dictionary of Music in Sound.

First published 2007 in Great Britain by
Rhinegold Publishing Ltd
241 Shaftesbury Avenue
London WC2H 8TF
Telephone: 020 7333 1720
Fax: 020 7333 1765
www.rhinegold.co.uk

You should always check the current requirements of the examination, since these may change.
Copies of the Edexcel Specification may be obtained from Edexcel Examinations at
Edexcel Publications, Adamsway, Mansfield, Nottinghamshire, NG18 4FN
Telephone: 01623 467467, Fax 01623 450481, Email publications@linneydirect.com
See also the Edexcel website at www.edexcel.org.uk

Lifelines Edexcel GCSE Music
British Library Cataloguing in Publication Data.
A catalogue record for this book is available from the British Library.

ISBN: 978-1-906178-01-7

Printed in Great Britain by WPG Ltd

CONTENTS

THE AUTHOR

Julia Winterson has more than 30 years experience of teaching in schools, colleges and universities. Her work as qualification leader for Edexcel involved the development of music specifications for Curriculum 2000. She is a member of the International Society of Contemporary Music British Committee and the Music Publishers Association Education and Training Group. She currently combines freelance writing with lecturing and research at the University of Huddersfield.

Julia Winterson's publications include the *Edexcel New Anthology of Music* (Peters Edition 2000), *The Edexcel GCSE Anthology of Music* (Peters Edition 2002), *The AQA GCSE Anthology of Music* (Peters Edition 2003), *Pop Music: The Text Book* (co-authored with Peter Nickol and Toby Bricheno, Peters Edition 2003), and *Pop Music: Question & Answer Book* (Peters Edition 2005).

ACKNOWLEDGEMENTS

The author would like to thank Paul Terry and Chrissy Porter for their advice and support during the preparation of this book. Thanks also to Elisabeth Boulton, Emma Findlow, Zöe Franklin, Nicola Goodman and Lucien Jenkins of Rhinegold Publishing for their assistance throughout the editing and production process.

Introduction

This Lifelines revision guide is designed to help you through the weeks leading up to the written listening examination for GCSE Music. More detailed notes about all aspects of the course are provided in *A Student's Guide to GCSE Music for the Edexcel Specification*, by David Bowman and Julia Winterson (Rhinegold Publishing 2006).

For your GCSE you have to **perform, compose,** and **listen and appraise.** This will involve being able to:

* Play and / or sing an individual part with technical control, expression, interpretation and, where appropriate, a sense of ensemble (performing)
* Create and develop musical ideas in relation to a set of detailed instructions (composing)
* Analyse and evaluate music using musical terminology (appraising).

You will study various kinds of music including:

* Classical music (Areas of Study 1 and 2)
* Popular music (Area of Study 3)
* Music from around the world (Area of Study 4).

GCSE MUSIC

Performing accounts for 30% of your GCSE			Percentage
(a)	Solo performance	You will perform one solo piece	15%
(b)	Ensemble performance	You will perform in, or direct, one ensemble piece	15%
Composing accounts for 30% of your GCSE			
(a)	Composition 1	One composition, written to a brief, based on one of the four Areas of Study	15%
(b)	Composition 2	Another composition, written to brief, but based on a different Area of Study	15%
Listening and appraising accounts for 40% of your GCSE			
(a)	Listening paper	A 1½ hour written paper containing questions based on all four Areas of Study	40%

Areas of Study

Area of Study 1	Area of Study 2	Area of Study 3	Area of Study 4
Structure in western classical music 1600–1899	Changing directions in western classical music from 1900	Popular music in context	Indian raga, African music and fusions
Topics	**Topics**	**Topics**	**Topics**
• Ground bass and variations • Ternary form • Rondo	• Expressionism and serialism • Minimalism • Experimental and electronic music	• Dance music 1985 – present day • Songs from musicals • Britpop and its influences	• Indian raga • African music • Fusions

The four Areas of Study form the backbone of Edexcel GCSE Music and connect the **performing, composing** and **listening and appraising** elements. You'll need a good knowledge of the stylistic features of the three topics in each Area of Study. What you learn in them can be used in your compositions and performances as well as in the Listening paper.

LISTENING PAPER

This book concentrates on the GCSE Listening Paper. If you are using it for the final summer exam you will probably have already completed the Composing and Performing papers.

In Paper 3 (Listening and Appraising) you will answer questions on eight extracts of music which will be played on CD in an examination lasting 1½ hours. Each extract will be repeated at least once, but you will not normally be given a score of the music. You may be asked to identify instruments, styles and technical features, and to describe the music (using technical terms). Each extract will come from one of the topics in the four Areas of Study. It is unlikely that the extracts will come from the specific pieces that you have studied in your lessons. However, in some questions, as well as being asked about the extract, you will also be asked for further information about the topic. Here you will be given marks for references to appropriate examples so you will get the chance to mention the pieces you have listened to in your lessons.

In order to do well in the exam you will need plenty of practice in answering questions on similar but unfamiliar pieces of music. Books of practice Listening Tests (with CDs) for this paper are produced by Rhinegold Publishing: *Listening Tests for Students for the Edexcel GCSE Music Specification, Books 1–3*.

There will be different types of question. Some will be multiple choice, whereas others will ask you to answer in your own words. Be prepared for both.

Ten top tips

Tactics are essential during the exam. Keep the following points in mind.

1. Read the questions carefully and make sure you understand what the examiner is looking for before you rush into writing your answer.

2. The paper has eight questions and goes through each Area of Study in turn: make sure you are aware of what information belongs in each topic and each Area of Study.

3. Look out for keywords in the questions (words such as device, tempo, dynamics, texture and tonality): these are likely to appear in the listening paper every year so you will need to be clear about what they mean.

4. Marks will be given for use of appropriate musical vocabulary: use the correct technical terms whenever you can; some credit will also be given for ordinary words which answer the questions adequately, so if you forget the 'right word', just get as close as you can.

5. Responses can often be single words, bullet points or short phrases; sentences are not required (but can be used).

6. If you are asked to underline or tick one answer in a multiple choice question, do not give more than one answer; anyone who does will automatically receive no marks for that question.

7. Don't be vague. Note the emphasis of questions and be clear in answering them; specify what you can hear by reference to an instrument or musical feature.

8. You will probably be asked to complete a melody and/or a rhythm so make sure that you know your intervals and time signatures.

9. You may start writing as soon as the music begins; it might be a good idea to pencil in your first thoughts and then to check their accuracy when you hear the music again.

10. Deal with each question as it comes: when it is over stop thinking about it and move on to the next one; you can always leave a mark next to the bit you are worried about and return to it at the end.

Structure in Western Classical Music 1600–1899

The form of a piece is usually based on repetition and contrast and normally falls into different sections. You will need to listen out for the different sections. These can be analysed using letter-names (A, B, C), where a new letter-name identifies a new section. Where a section is a variation on the previous one, use A¹ A² A³ where 1, 2 and 3 represent variations on theme A.

Most music has some repetition and some variety. Here are some common structures. You will need to know all of these for this part of the exam.

Ground bass	A¹	A²	A³	A⁴				
Variations	A¹	A²	A³	A⁴				
Ternary form	A	B	A					Three-part form
Rondo	A	B	A	C	A	D	A	Other patterns (such as ABACABA) are equally common.

Some composers add an introduction and ending (coda) to the forms above.

GROUND BASS AND VARIATIONS

Ground bass

A **ground bass** is a repeating bass line (known as **basso ostinato** in Italian) which forms the basis of a set of continuous melodic and / or harmonic variations. The bass line repeats many times. It can be long or short, but it does not usually have less than four notes. The variations usually get more and more complex as the piece goes on.

A **canon** is a musical device where the theme is played first by one instrument (the leader) and then imitated a few beats later by another instrument while the leader continues, and so on. (Think of *Three Blind Mice*.)

The bass line of Pachelbel's famous canon has eight notes that are repeated throughout the piece – 28 times in all [NGAM page 8 CD1 track 2].

The ground bass was most popular during the **baroque** period (c1600–1750). A keyboard instrument (such as the harpsichord) can often be heard playing the continuo part in most music of this period.

A **continuo** is a bass part found in baroque music from which accompanying chords are usually improvised on a harmony instrument such as harpsichord, organ or lute. The bass line is usually played on a cello, double bass or bassoon.

The baroque composer Purcell wrote a lot of music which uses a ground bass. 'The Plainte' is a lament taken from his stage work *The Fairy Queen*. The music is both sad and beautiful. It has a seven-bar ground bass that uses a lot of semitones [NGAM page 6 CD1 track 1].

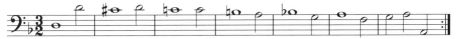

Purcell also composed what is probably the most famous ground bass piece ever written – 'Dido's Lament' [NAM page 356–358 CD3 track 14]. The first six notes of the ground descend **chromatically** from the tonic to the dominant.

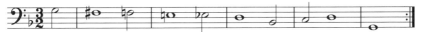

Variations

Variations are built upon a theme (a main melody). The piece opens with the statement of a simple theme which is then repeated several times with various alterations to one or more of its original elements. Variations sometimes take a well-known melody as their starting point.

There are many ways in which a theme can be varied and developed. Composers can:

* Decorate or ornament the melody
* Put the theme in the bass and the chords over the top (or vice versa)
* Put the theme in an inner part
* Turn the theme upside down (inversion)
* Use the theme backwards (retrograde)
* Imitate the theme among the parts
* Make the notes of the theme longer (augmentation)
* Make the notes of the theme shorter (diminution)
* Add rests
* Add a drone or a pedal note
* Change the accompaniment
* Add an ostinato
* Change the key signature (perhaps going from minor to major or vice versa)
* Change the time signature, for example from $\frac{4}{4}$ to $\frac{3}{4}$
* Change the harmony
* Change the instruments
* Change the tempo

◆ Change the articulation (legato to staccato and so on)

◆ Change the rhythm (dotted, syncopated and so on) rhythms.

Composers of the baroque and classical (c.1750–1825) periods often used **melodic decoration** in their variations. This means that the original melody is decorated with:

◆ Ornaments (trills, turns, mordents and so on)

◆ Passing notes (extra notes between the original notes)

◆ Scalic passages

◆ Arpeggios.

Later on composers often used **motivic development** in their variations. A motif is a short musical idea. It might have as few as two or three notes that contain one or more intervals and a characteristic rhythm.

With this type of development, motifs from the theme are repeated, varied and combined in new patterns; a whole variation may be built upon one short idea.

Beethoven uses motivic development in his solo piano piece the *Diabelli Variations* [GAM page 25 CD1 tracks 4–8]. The piece has a fairly simple waltz theme (written by Diabelli and passed to several composer friends to see what they could do with it) which is transformed from one variation to another as he concentrates on one or two ideas he has taken from the theme. In Variation 1, Beethoven changes it into a march partly by changing the time signature and slowing down the tempo.

Test yourself on ground bass and variations

1. Complete the table by writing the name of a form in the first column to show which forms are represented by the letter-names. You will see that two of them are the same – you will need to think of two different forms for these two.

Form							
	A	B	A	C	A	D	A
	A	B	A				
	A^1	A^2	A^3	A^4			
	A^1	A^2	A^3	A^4			

2. List six ways in which a composer can vary and develop a theme.
3. What is meant by melodic decoration?
4. What is meant by motivic development?
5. Write the name of the correct musical period (baroque, classical or romantic) next to each of these sets of dates.

	Roughly 1600–1750
	Roughly 1825–1900
	Roughly 1750–1825

Musical vocabulary test

Explain what is meant by each of the following:
* Imitation
* Canon
* Ostinato
* Augmentation
* Pedal note
* Articulation
* Continuo.

TERNARY FORM

Ternary form is a simple three-part structure (ABA) in which the first and last sections are identical or very similar, with a contrasting middle section. It is a musical sandwich where the outer A sections are the bread and the middle B section is the filling.

A	B	A
First section (tonic key)	Contrasting section (often in a related key)	Repetition of first section (ends in tonic key)

The first section usually ends with a perfect cadence. The second A section may be an exact repetition of the first A section or it may be slightly different, perhaps a little shorter.

Composers achieve contrast in the middle section through changes in:
* Harmony
* Rhythm
* Dynamics
* Tempo
* Texture
* Key.

In your exam you may be asked to describe ways in which the middle section contrasts with the outer sections. So it is a good idea to practise spotting differences between the sections when you are listening to a piece in ternary form.

Ternary form is a structure often associated with western classical music, especially during the baroque, classical and romantic eras.

Da capo aria

The da capo aria is a ternary structure used in baroque vocal music. The third section of the piece is not written out: instead, the composer ends the middle section (B) with the words 'Da capo' (Italian: 'from the beginning'), indicating that the first section (A) should then be repeated. The singer usually improvises ornaments during the A-section repeat. For example, listen to 'He was despised' from *Messiah* by Handel [GAM page 52 CD1 track 24].

A	B	A
First section	A contrasting section	First section repeated but now decorated with ornaments.

Minuet and trio

Minuet and trio is a ternary structure used in symphonies, string quartets and sonatas of the classical period. This form is often the basis of a third movement of a work, usually in triple time. For example, listen to Mozart's Symphony No 40, movement III [GAM page 56 CD1 track 25].

A	B	A
Minuet	Trio (a contrasting section in a different key)	Minuet

Miniature

The piano miniature (meaning short piece) made use of ternary structure and was popular during the romantic period. Often a single-movement work, composers associated with the form are Chopin, Grieg, Mendelssohn and Schumann. For example, listen to *Little Folksong* by Schumann [NGAM page 29 CD1 track 4].

Test yourself on ternary form

1. Explain why a minuet and trio could be described as being in ternary form.
2. Describe three ways in which composers can achieve contrast in the middle section of ternary form.
3. What is meant by da capo?
4. What is a perfect cadence?

RONDO

The structure of rondo form is:

A	B	A	C	A	etc

Rondos are often used as the last movement in classical symphonies and concertos. Here are some key points:

- First section (A) returns several times throughout the movement – the main theme keeps coming round (hence rondo)
- The A section is sometimes known as the refrain
- Refrains are separated from each other by contrasting passages known as episodes

- The refrain is usually in the tonic key
- Episodes may be in different but related keys.

When a passage changes key it is said to have modulated. **Related keys** are those which share many common notes with the original key. In any major key the closely related keys are the dominant, subdominant and the relative minor. The relative keys for C major are shown below.

Tonic	C major
Subdominant	F major
Dominant	G major
Relative minor	A minor

Sometimes there will be links between the sections and occasionally a coda (closing section) is added.

Composers achieve contrast in the episodes through changes in:

- Melody
- Harmony
- Rhythm
- Dynamics
- Tempo
- Texture
- Key
- Instrumentation.

In your exam you may be asked to describe ways in which the episodes contrast with the outer sections. It is a good idea to practise spotting differences between the refrain and the episodes when you are listening to a piece in rondo form. Here are some rondos from different periods that you could listen to: *Les Moissonneurs* by Couperin [NGAM page 32 CD1 track 6]; Clarinet Quintet in B♭, movement IV by Weber [GAM page 40 CD1 track 2]; and *Pavane pour une infante défunte* by Ravel [NGAM page 34 CD1 track 7] .

Test yourself on rondo form

1. Describe the structure of a rondo.
2. What is the refrain of a rondo?
3. Give three ways in which composers achieve contrast in the episodes.

Musical vocabulary test

Explain what is meant by each of the following.

- Modulation
- Related key
- Coda.

Changing Directions in Western Classical Music from 1900

The 20th century was an exciting period in music. It was a time of changing directions, exploration and experiment, leading to a variety of new styles and sounds. You will need to know about the following styles:

* Expressionism
* Serialism
* Minimalism
* Experimental and electronic music.

EXPRESSIONISM

One of the first new styles to appear in the 20th century was expressionism. The term expressionism was originally borrowed from visual art and literature. Artists created vivid pictures, distorting colours and shapes to express their innermost, sometimes nightmarish emotions. In a similar way, composers poured intense emotional expression into their music exploring their dark subconscious. An example of expressionist painting is *The Scream* (1893) by Norwegian artist Edvard Munch. Type 'The Scream' into www.wikipedia.org or visit www.edvard-munch.com.

Expressionist music largely avoids:

* Cadence
* Repetition
* Sequence
* Balanced phrases.

Expressionist music often:

* Has a high level of dissonance
* Contains extreme contrasts of dynamics
* Has constantly changing textures and ideas
* Includes distorted melodies and harmonies
* Has instruments playing at the extremes of their ranges
* Has angular melodies with wide leaps
* Has very chromatic harmonies.

The harmony in expressionist music is often very chromatic. As harmonies became increasingly chromatic, the sense of key became less and less obvious eventually resulting in **atonality**.

Two important expressionist composers are **Schoenberg** and **Berg**.

Alban Berg's opera *Wozzeck* is a work of expressionism [NGAM page 46 CD1 tracks 9–11]. It is a true murder story that depicts the extreme emotional state of the title character and his descent into madness. The nightmarish events in the story are underlined by the music used to express Wozzeck's hallucinations and isolation. Because of the complex chromaticism, angular melodies and atonal harmonies, there is no real sense of key.

Arnold Schoenberg's song cycle *Pierrot Lunaire* (1912) is both atonal and expressionist [NGAM page 46 CD1 track 8]. It is a weird and powerful work revealing different aspects of the moonstruck hero, Pierrot. It is for female reciter and a chamber ensemble of five players. The voice part uses **Sprechgesang** (German for 'speech-song' and sometimes called Sprechstimme) – this is an eerily expressive technique halfway between singing and speaking. 'Valse de Chopin' compares a Chopin waltz to a drop of blood staining the lips of someone who is dying. The music is in triple time, like a waltz, but it is distorted, with angular melodic lines, dissonant harmonies and complex **counterpoint**.

SERIALISM

Schoenberg eventually evolved a new system to replace tonality in his music. This was called serialism or the 12-note system. The three most well-known serialist composers are **Arnold Schoenberg, Alban Berg** and **Anton Webern**. Together they are known as the **Second Viennese School**.

How does serialism work?

First of all a composer creates a **note row** or **tone row**; this is a sequence that uses all 12 notes of the chromatic scale. None of the notes are repeated in the tone row (also known as the **prime order** or prime series) until all 12 pitches have been used. The note row is the basis of the whole composition. There are four main ways of using the row. Below is the note row (prime order) of the Trio from the Minuet of the *Suite for Piano* Op 25 by Schoenberg [NGAM page 54 CD1 track 12].

Prime Order

Note row, tone row, prime row and prime order all mean the same thing.

Inversion

The whole row can be turned upside down or inverted. This is known as an inversion.

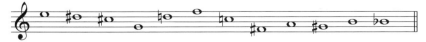

Retrograde

The original note row can be played backwards as a retrograde.

Retrograde inversion

The inversion can itself be played backwards as a retrograde inversion.

Other things composers can do to vary a note row:

- All four versions of the row can be transposed to start on any note of the chromatic scale
- Notes can be used vertically to make chords: verticalisation
- Note durations can be lengthened, for example crotchets become minims: augmentation
- Note durations can be shortened, for example crotchets become quavers: diminution
- Notes can be used in another octave: octave displacement.

Two devices not unique to serialist music but often used are **imitation** and **canon**:

- Imitation: a short melodic idea in one part is copied by another part while the melodic line of the first part continues
- Canon: the theme is played first by one instrument (the leader) and then imitated exactly a few beats later by another instrument, while the first part continues to unfold. The two parts sometimes continue in this manner for an entire piece.

In serialism the pitch of the notes is strictly controlled. Some composers went on to write music where every aspect of the music (such as rhythm and dynamics) was controlled by the principles of serialism. This is known as **total serialism**.

Some composers who have used total serialism are Karlheinz Stockhausen, Pierre Boulez and Milton Babbitt.

Test yourself on expressionism and serialism

1. Where did musicians borrow the term expressionism from?
2. Describe some of the ways in which expressionist composers portray intense emotion in their music.
3. What was the Second Viennese School? Name three prominent members.
4. Give two other names for a note row.
5. Describe four ways that a note row might be used.
6. What is meant by total serialism?
7. Name two composers who have used total serialism.

Musical vocabulary test

Explain what is meant by each of the following terms?
* Atonality
* Chromatic harmony
* Counterpoint
* Sprechstimme
* Note row
* Retrograde inversion
* Octave displacement
* Canon
* Imitation.

MINIMALISM

Minimalist music features constantly repeated patterns that are subjected to gradual processes of melodic and rhythmic change (transformation) as the piece develops. A layered texture is often used, and the harmony is frequently **diatonic**. The effect can be almost hypnotic.

Expressionism and serialism were both at the cutting edge of 20th-century music, and are both complex modernist styles which are often dissonant and atonal. In contrast, minimalism is simple and tonal. It appeared after the modernist styles and so can be referred to as post-modernist.

Minimalism originated on the west coast of America in the 1960s with composers including **Terry Riley**, **Steve Reich** and **Philip Glass**. Terry Riley wrote his minimalist classic *In C* in 1964 [GAM page 71–72 CD2 track 4]. It is made up of 53 music motifs, roughly one bar each. The piece is written for any number of instruments, with one musician playing continuous quaver Cs on the piano to keep time. The 53 melodic fragments are played in order: each muscian decides how many times to repeat each motif before moving on to the next. Each performance will have a different outcome because of the improvisatory nature.

In C has many of the characteristics of minimalist music:

* **Tonal** (key of C in this case)
* Lots of repetition
* Layers of **ostinati** (the plural of ostinato)
* Interlocking repeated phrases and rhythms
* Gradual changes
* Unvarying pulse.

Minimalist music often uses:

* Arpeggios and broken chords (where the notes of a chord are played singly rather than together)
* Phase shifting
* Addition and subtraction (where notes are added to, or taken away from a repeated phrase)
* Melodic transformation (where a melody gradually changes shape)
* Rhythmic transformation (where a rhythm gradually changes shape)
* Gradual changes in texture
* Gradual changes in dynamics such as long crescendos or diminuendos.

In phase shifting (or phasing) one part repeats constantly while another gradually shifts out of phase with it. *Clapping Music* by Steve Reich [GAM page 72–73 CD2 track 3] uses phase shifting:

* Two performers clap the same short phrase
* One performer gradually shifts further out of phase with the other by starting on a different beat of the pattern
* Eventually the parts come together again.

The most well-known minimalist composers are Terry Riley, Steve Reich, Philip Glass and John Adams [NGAM page 56 CD1 track 13].

Test yourself on minimalism

1. Where and when did minimalism originate?
2. Explain what each of these minimalist techniques mean:
   * Phase shifting
   * Melodic transformation
   * Addition and subtraction.
3. How would you describe the texture of minimalist music?
4. Name two well-known minimalist composers.

Musical vocabulary test

What is meant by each of the following:
* Arpeggio
* Tonal
* Crescendo
* Ostinati.

EXPERIMENTAL AND ELECTRONIC MUSIC

Experimental music

The American composer John Cage (1912–1992) is one of the most important figures in 20th-century music. He believed that any object could be used to make music, and any noise could be music. Experimental music questions what music is and asks 'What could music also be?'

The most famous piece of experimental music ever written is John Cage's *4'33"*. It is a three-movement work where each movement is marked *'Tacet'*. The performer is asked to make no sounds at all – for any length of time on any instrument. This turns the idea of concert music on its head.

Cage wanted to give up control so that 'sounds can be sounds'. He was fascinated by **aleatoric** (or indeterminate) **music**, which uses chance operations (such as tossing a coin or rolling a dice to determine which notes to play) bringing about unpredictable outcomes. Aleatoric music is different every time it is performed.

Graphic scores

Conventional staff notation cannot always cope with the demands of experimental and electronic music, so some composers used new systems such as **graphic notation** and **prose scores** (where a descriptive list of musical events is given). Graphic scores use diagrams, pictures and symbols to indicate how the piece is to be performed. Two famous examples of graphic scores are *Treatise* by Cornelius Cardew and *Stripsody* by Cathy Berberian. (You can see two pages from *Treatise* in GAM page 81–82.)

The score of 'The Lady in Waiting' from *Eight Songs for a Mad King* by Peter Maxwell Davis uses musical staves, but they are arranged in a pattern which looks like a bird cage [NGAM page 60 CD1 track 14].

Stripsody and *Eight Songs for a Mad King* both use extended vocal techniques. This is where unusual and unexpected sounds are created by the voice such as panting, whistling, hissing or barking.

Extended instrumental techniques are the methods used when traditional instruments are played in unusual ways in order to produce new sounds. Here are some examples:

* **Multiphonics**: two or more notes are played at the same time on an instrument that is designed to produce only

one note at a time; this can be done through special fingerings and changes to the lip position

◆ **Singing** and **speaking** into the instrument

◆ **Quartertones**: intervals half the size of a semitone

◆ **Note bending**: sounding a pitch and then altering the note up / down a quartertone

◆ **Flutter tonguing**: blowing a wind or brass instrument while trilling the tongue.

There are also various new ways of sounding percussion instruments, for example bowing xylophones and dipping cymbals in water.

A **prepared piano** is a piano that has had its sound altered by inserting objects (such as nuts, bolts and screws), between, under and over the piano strings. This produces some weird and wonderful sounds.

Unconventional instruments – some composers have experimented with the sound possibilities of different objects and materials creating junk percussion bands and sound sculptures.

Electronic music

Electronic music uses sounds that are generated and / or manipulated electronically. An electronic piece may:

◆ Use only electronically generated sounds, sometimes pre-recorded and then manipulated live before an audience

◆ Combine electronic sounds with instruments or voices; these may then be transformed electronically, either live or on tape; this is known as electro-acoustic music.

The first milestone in the development of electronic music was the invention of magnetic recording tape. In the 1940s the composer Pierre Schaeffer experimented with making musical collages using natural and man-made sounds. This became known as **musique concrète**. The sounds were recorded on tape and the tapes were then manipulated in different ways, being played:

◆ At different speeds

◆ Backwards

◆ Spliced (cut up)

◆ Looped (where a short section of tape sound is repeated over and over again)

◆ Superimposed on top of each other.

Such techniques transformed the sounds dramatically, producing new timbres and effects. Twenty years later such techniques were introduced into pop music by George Martin and the Beatles, on *Sergeant Pepper's Lonely Hearts Club Band*.

In the 1950s, studios began to use oscillators, amplifiers and signal-processing devices to generate sounds electronically. In 1963 the BBC Radiophonic Workshop produced one of the most well-known pieces of electronic music ever, the original theme music for *Dr Who*.

In 1955 the first **synthesiser** was developed at the RCA studios in New York. It was programmed by punched paper tape and occupied a whole room. (A synthesiser is a device which generates sounds electronically.)

One of the most well-known composers to create electronic music is Stockhausen. His 1956 piece *Gesang der Jünglinge* (Song of Youth) combines the sound of a boy's voice with pure electronic sound.

Below are some of the ways in which sounds can be manipulated electronically:

◆ **Chorus**: an effect created by taking an audio signal and mixing it with several delayed copies of itself, sounding as though there are several instruments / voices where there is really only one

◆ **Delay**: any type of effect that adds a delayed version of the original signal, to create effects such as **reverb** or **echo**

◆ The beginning of sounds (**attack**) and the endings of sounds (**decay**) may be changed

◆ **Filtering**: cutting out unwanted frequencies.

Many of these are used in *Vox 5* by Trevor Wishart [GAM page 89 CD2 track 12] and *A Passing Phase* by Nye Parry [NGAM page 66 CD1 track 16].

The system of recording in use before the 1980s was known as **analogue recording**, so called because the recorded signal is stored in patterns which correspond with (or are analogous to) the waveforms of the original sound.

Digital technology (in which sounds are stored and manipulated as a series of complex numbers) opened up a whole new range of creative possibilities in the 1980s. MIDI (Musical Instrument Digital Interface) was introduced in 1983 to enable electronic instruments to be connected together and used in conjunction with each other.

Digital technology led to the commerial development of samplers and sequencers in the 1980s:

◆ **A sampler**: can store any audio sound, process it and play it back

◆ **A sample**: a digitally recorded fragment of sound taken from a pre-existing source for use in a new piece; sampled sounds are often used in synthesisers and on computers

◆ **A sequencer**: designed for inputting, editing, storing and playing back data from a musical performance.

Test yourself on experimental and electronic music

1. How does a graphic score work?
2. What are extended instrumental techniques?
3. Describe how a piano can be prepared.
4. Explain what is meant by musique concrète.
5. What is electro-acoustic music?
6. Describe some of the ways in which music can be manipulated electronically.
7. What does MIDI stand for?

Musical vocabulary test

Explain what is meant by each of the following:
* Tacet
* Sampler
* Sequencer
* Synthesiser
* Multiphonics
* Aleatoric music
* Analogue recording.

Area of Study 3
Popular Music in Context

Popular music is, according to the specification, being studied 'in context', but don't let that fool you into studying non-musical topics. Here, as elsewhere, there will be questions about instruments, technology, form and structure, rhythms, harmonies – the music itself, not the celebrity lifestyle.

There are three topics:
- Dance Music 1985–Present Day
- Songs from Musicals
- Britpop and its Influences.

DANCE MUSIC 1985–PRESENT DAY

Modern dance music is technology-based, with the DJ often playing an important role in mixing and presenting tracks. It is characterised by:
- Four-on-the-floor rhythms
- Extensive use of samples and loops
- New technology
- Layered textures.

Roots of dance music

- **Jamaican dub** (originated 1970s): a style of reggae in which new instrumental versions of songs are made by remixing existing recordings adding effects such as echo and reverb, for example Lee Scratch Perry
- **Funk** (originated 1970s): jazzy, energetic, dominated by guitars and groove-based (long sections with the same rhythm parts are repeated for dancing), for example Sly and the Family Stone and James Brown
- **Disco** (originated 1970s): a type of up-tempo dance music which emerged in the early 1970s. It combined four-on-the-floor rhythms, raucous energy and luscious orchestral arrangements, for example Donna Summer's *I Feel Love*, the first hit song to have an entirely synthesised backing track [NGAM page 70 CD2 track 3]
- **Electro-pop** (originated 1980s): used lots of electronic instruments, for example Kraftwerk, Pet Shop Boys and Depeche Mode.

Dance music styles

Hip-hop: features DJs, MCs and rap. Some hip-hop DJs extended the breaks of records by mixing two copies of the same record.

House music takes its name from Chicago's arehouse club. In the 1980s, DJ Frankie Knuckles anipulated recordings, lengthening some sections, emphasising and repeating others.

He added pre-set percussion patterns to emphasise the solid beats which were soon to define house music. Musical characteristics of house music include:

- Four-on-the-floor bass drum
- Samples
- Repetitive synthesiser riffs
- Drum rolls
- Off-beat hi-hat patterns
- It may include vocals (or vocal samples) and piano chords
- Tempo usually around 120 bpm.

Techno has similar drum patterns to house, but with more use of purely synthetic sounds. There is often little or no chord movement. Tempo is usually around 120−140 bpm.

Trance is an offshoot of techno but with more emphasis on harmony and with much use of synthesisers. Tempo is usually around 120−150 bpm.

Musical characteristics of **drum and bass / jungle**:

- A drum loop
- A heavy bass line
- Often speeded-up hip-hop breaks
- Often high-speed retriggering of the drums (see definition on page 26)
- Tempo usually around 170 bpm.

Garage uses house loops combined with synthesised bass lines. The tempo is usually around 120 bpm.

DJs

Disc jockies (**DJs**) originated in America about 70 years ago as radio presenters who selected and played recordings. Much later DJs were used in dance clubs, initially with a similar role, but then imposing their own personalities beyond the choice of discs, to add commentary to the music and event. Dance music DJs use different ways to manipulate the sound, adding their own creative element to the music they play. Originally DJs used vinyl records, but today many use CD decks, laptops and software packages to cut up tracks, loop sections and add new parts as part of the performance. DJ techniques include:

- **Mixing**: two discs are mixed together through beat-matching and sometimes pitch control
- **Beatmatching:** a mixing technique which involves changing the speed at which a disc is played so that its tempo matches that of the song currently playing
- **Pitch control:** a technique used to alter the pitch of a song and enable a smooth mix into another song of the same pitch; it can also be used to alter the pitch of sections of a song

- Scratching: moving a disc back and forth while it is playing to manipulate the original sound
- Cueing: finding a suitable point in a song for the DJ to mix in a new track.

Dance music technology

In the 1970s, the first Technics SL1200 turntable had a big impact in dance clubs: it lent itself to scratching. A pitch control was added enabling the user to speed up or slow down records. This meant two records could be **beat matched** and songs could be mixed together.

The introduction of **MIDI** in the early 1980s enabled one musician to control many different electronic instruments easily and cheaply. The main devices and processes are:

- **Synthesiser**: generates sounds electronically
- **Sequencer**: for inputting, editing, storing and playing back data from a musical performance
- **Sampler**: processes, manipulates and plays back audio material
- **Sample**: a digitally recorded fragment of sound, for example a guitar riff, a verse of a song, the sound of rain drops, indeed anything; sampled sounds are often played through synthesisers and software sequencers
- **Vocoder**: a sound processor which distorts the human voice to sound synthetic with a robotic effect
- **Drum machines**: Roland CR and TR drum machines were the first to have programmable rhythms; drum machines have largely been replaced by computer-based sequencers using sampled drum sounds
- **Remixing**: record producers take an original multi-track recording and make a new version by changing the style and balance; they usually add new parts and take away ingredients of the original, for example the three remixes of *Spellbound* by Rae and Christian [GAM page 99–102 CD3 tracks 5–7]
- **Chorus**: an effect created by taking an audio signal and mixing it with several delayed copies of itself – it sounds as though there are several instruments or voices where there is really only one
- **Delay**: any type of effect that adds a delayed version of the original signal, to create effects such as reverb or echo
- **EQ**: short for equalisation, where sound frequencies are either boosted or reduced to create a desired sound – dance music often uses powerful low-bass frequencies
- **Reverb**: short for reverberation – it can be created artificially in recording and is the most commonly used studio effect
- **Retriggering**: an effect produced when a sample is constantly re-activated
- **Panning**: the positioning of a sound in the stereo field – it may be used to give the impression that the sound is moving from side to side, or it may stay fixed on, for example the left, right or centre of the overall mix.

The structure of dance music

Many dance tracks could be described as collages where a series of episodes (often samples and loops) are layered over a foundation of drums and bass. The main sections of dance music can usually be identified as:

* **Mix in**: the opening section where the DJ can mix the previous track into the new one – usually a drum or percussion section

* **Breakdown**: the sounds drop out in order to create tension when they later build up again

* **Mix out**: the closing section where the DJ can start to mix in the next track – a drum or percussion section.

Test yourself on dance music

1. What are the main musical characteristics of dance music?
2. Describe some of the roots of today's dance music.
3. Write a sentence about each of the following styles:
    * Trance
    * Garage
    * House.
4. Describe three DJ techniques commonly used.
5. What is the difference between a sampler and a synthesiser?

Music vocabulary test

Explain what is meant by each of the following:
* Sample
* Loop
* Reverb
* Breakdown
* Mix out
* Retriggering
* EQ
* Reverb.

SONGS FROM MUSICALS

What is a musical?

Musicals set out to entertain through a combination of:

* Catchy music in a popular style
* Solo songs, duets, choruses, ensembles and dance music
* Orchestral or band accompaniment

- Spoken dialogue
- Stage spectacles and magnificent costumes.

These are all held together by the plot. Every musical has a:

- **Libretto**: the overall text including the spoken and sung parts
- **Lyrics**: the words to the songs.

Songs

Most songs are either action songs which move the plot forward or character songs which enable a character to express their feelings. Within these two formats, different song types can be found:

- **Ballads** are usually slow, romantic and reflective
- **Comedy songs** are funny, so the lyrics are very important, for example 'I cain't say no' from *Oklahoma!* [NGAM page 72 CD2 track 4]
- **Production numbers** involving the full company often open and close acts, and are used to show major changes in location or plot, for example 'Oklahoma' from *Oklahoma!* (Rodgers and Hammerstein) [NGAM page 76 CD2 track 5], 'The ballad of Sweeney Todd' from *Sweeney Todd* (Stephen Sondheim) [NGAM page 86 CD2 track 6] and 'Consider Yourself' from *Oliver* (Lionel Bart) [GAM page 104 CD3 track 9]
- **Rhythm songs** are driven by energetic rhythm patterns.

Although most musicals use dialogue, some are **through-composed**. This means that there is little spoken dialogue and nearly everything is sung.

Which song forms do you find in musicals?

The 32-bar song uses a chorus in AABA form with each section usually being eight bars long.

A	Melody 1
	Chord sequence 1
A	Melody 1 (either identical or with some slight variation)
	Chord sequence 1
B	Middle-eight (or bridge)
	Contrasting melody 2
	Chord sequence 2
A	Melody 1 (either identical or with some slight variation)
	Chord sequence 1

The middle-eight is a contrasting section, often with a different arrangement of instruments and / or different chords. The words may also have a different subject.

The 32-bar song may be extended to include an:

♦ **Intro**: an opening section consisting of an instrumental introduction and / or a sung verse before the main 32-bar chorus

♦ **Outro**: a concluding section also known as coda

♦ Instrumental interlude.

Other common song forms used in shows are ABAC form, ABAB form, and verse-and-chorus form.

In **verse-and-chorus** form:

♦ The **chorus** sets the refrain of the lyrics and often contains the title words; it usually returns several times, always with the same words, and is normally the catchiest part of the song

♦ The **verse** usually has different words with each repetition – the rhyming scheme and the musical scheme may have a different form. For example, the rhyme scheme might be AABB but the musical form might be ABAC – so don't rely on the words to indicate the structure of the music.

The history of the musical

18th century: John Gay's *Beggar's Opera* (1728) is a piece of musical theatre using popular songs of the day, known then as a **ballad opera**.

19th century: European **operetta** used music, spoken dialogue, light subject matter, comedy elements and romance. The main centres for operetta were Vienna (Franz Léhar and Johann Strauss), Paris (Jacques Offenbach) and London (Gilbert and Sullivan).

Early 20th century: Early musicals were usually **musical comedies** or **revues**. Revues were very popular in American theatres. They were a form of variety show featuring musical numbers, comedy sketches and novelty acts. The most famous of these were the Ziegfeld Follies.

1920s and 1930s: The popular music publishing industry was in New York and was known as **Tin Pan Alley**. The most successful Tin Pan Alley songwriters are the 'Big Five' – Irving Berlin, George Gershwin, Jerome Kern, Cole Porter and Richard Rodgers. Their music was often jazzy and written for **Broadway** musicals. (Broadway is a street in New York where many musicals are staged. It is also used as a general term to refer to American musicals.)

Some famous musicals

Show Boat (1927, music by Jerome Kern, libretto and lyrics by Oscar Hammerstein) tells the story of Mississippi riverboat entertainers. It was probably the first musical to integrate the music and lyrics, and could be described as a play with music rather than a musical comedy.

Porgy and Bess (1935, George Gershwin). This jazzy musical is sometimes described as an American folk opera. One of the songs it features is 'Summertime', now a jazz standard.

Oklahoma! (1942, Richard Rodgers and Oscar Hammerstein). The dance, music, and drama were amalgamated into a dramatic unity. Rodgers and Hammerstein had a string of hits including *Carousel*, *South Pacific*, *The King and I* and *The Sound of Music*.

West Side Story (1957, music by Leonard Bernstein and words by Stephen Sondheim), a musical using a more contemporary jazz style, based on Shakespeare's *Romeo and Juliet* but the tragic love story is updated to 20th-century New York against a background of gang warfare.

Stephen Sondheim went on to write innovative musicals of his own including (during the 1970s) *A Little Night Music*, *Company* and *Sweeney Todd: The Demon Barber of Fleet Street*.

Hair (1966) launched the rock musical with its flower power and hippies, rude words and nudity (music composed by Galt MacDermot). Other rock based musicals of the same era include *Grease* and *Tommy*.

Andrew Lloyd Webber has had a stream of successes since 1970 including *Jesus Christ Superstar*, *Evita*, *Cats* and *Sunset Boulevard*. His musicals have fabulous costumes and sets, and often contain a spectacular scenic element such as the falling chandelier in *Phantom of the Opera* or the rail track in *Starlight Express*.

Test yourself on musicals

1. What are the main ingredients of a musical?
2. Name three different types of songs that you might find in a musical. Give a short description of their characteristics.
3. Write a paragraph about the origins of the musical.
4. Describe the structure of 32-bar song form. Give an example of a song that uses this form.
5. What is a middle-eight?
6. What is the difference between a verse and a chorus?
7. What is meant by Tin Pan Alley?
8. What is meant by Broadway?

Musical vocabulary test

Explain what is meant by each of the following:
+ Libretto
+ Lyrics
+ Production number
+ Intro
+ Outro
+ Action song
+ Character song
+ Operetta.

BRITPOP AND ITS INFLUENCES

What is Britpop?

Britpop was a reaction against the American and electronic dance music styles of the early 1990s. It looked back to the 1960s for inspiration and such British groups as the Kinks, the Who, the Small Faces and the Beatles. This term describes British bands such as **Oasis, Blur,** and **Pulp**. Britpop music is characterised by:

♦ The use of live guitarists and drummers rather than sequenced electronic sounds

♦ A traditional line-up of lead guitar, bass guitar, drums and vocals

♦ Verse and chorus songs

♦ Strong melodies

♦ Conventional chord patterns.

Influences

The Beatles are the most successful pop band ever. Every album was a huge hit, with perhaps two of the best being *Revolver* (1966) and *Sgt Pepper's Lonely Hearts Club Band* (1967). They helped to create a distinctly British sound which used:

♦ Natural (rather than fake American) accents

♦ Standard song forms

♦ Distinctive chord patterns and vocal harmonies

♦ Rhythmic guitar work

♦ Simple melodies

♦ Clever lyrics.

John Lennon and Paul McCartney wrote most of their own material. George Martin was their imaginative producer and arranger. The Beatles had a huge influence and pop groups sprang up all over the UK usually writing their own songs.

The Kinks were a four-piece band who had a string of hits during the 1960s including *Waterloo Sunset*, *Sunny Afternoon* and *Dedicated Follower of Fashion* [NGAM page 100 CD2 track 8]. Their songs were short and punchy with thought-provoking lyrics and elements of music hall. Songwriter Ray Davies' lyrics often used images of everyday English life.

The **Small Faces** 1960s hits included *Lazy Sunday*, *All or Nothing* and *Itchycoo Park*. They were Eastenders which comes across in their songs, in both the imagery and in Steve Marriott's Cockney accent. Their songs too have a music hall flavour and often include sing-along choruses.

All these groups helped to establish a British tradition of guitar-based pop groups playing verse-and-chorus songs, rich in hooks and with plenty of melodic interest. Britpop bands drew on these 1960s characteristics, sometimes even borrowing words and melodies.

The Manchester sound

Britpop bands were also influenced by the Smiths, the Stone Roses and Happy Mondays who all hailed from Manchester in the 1980s and 1990s. The music of the Smiths:

◆ Is based on standard verse-and-chorus pop structures

◆ Has a classic four piece line-up of vocal, guitars and drums

◆ Has witty lyrics often about unrequited love in everyday northern England.

Two of the best known bands of the later 'Madchester' scene were the Stone Roses and the Happy Mondays. The music often introduced elements of house music and was influenced by the music of the 1960s, particularly Beatles psychedelia.

Oasis' first album, *Definitely Maybe* (1994), entered the charts at No 1. The original four piece line-up featured two guitars, vocals and drums: similar to the line-up that would have been used in the 1960s. Listen to *Don't Look Back in Anger* [NAM 57 CD4 track 15]. Oasis have a very distinctive sound, a dense texture with rhythmic guitars. They were much influenced by the Beatles, the Smiths and the Sex Pistols. The influence of the Beatles can be heard in the:

◆ Distinctive melodies following in Lennon and McCartney's songwriting style

◆ Main interest in the vocal line

◆ Quotations from Beatles's songs

◆ Vocal harmonies

◆ Borrowed chord sequences.

The influence of punk rock, such as the Sex Pistols, can be heard in the strident guitar sound and the sometimes brash, sneering vocals.

Blur were the rivals of Oasis during the 1990s. Blur were great fans of the Kinks. They had a line-up of vocalist, guitar, bass guitar and drums but with added keyboards. Their albums *Modern Life is Rubbish* and *Parklife* invoked Englishness – Sunday roasts and Saturday markets – in the same way that the Kinks' albums had done 30 years earlier. For example, *Charmless Man* [NGAM page 96 CD2 track 7].

Verse and chorus form

Intro (Introduction)	The opening section of a song: it could be a repeated riff, a few strummed guitar chords, or one of the main melodies. It is designed to catch the attention of the listener.
Verse	A section of melody which is repeated each time with different words. The storyline of the song is usually found in the verse. The melody and chord progressions usually remain the same in each verse. The verse alternates with the chorus.
Chorus	A setting of the refrain of the lyrics, often containing the title words of the song and sometimes the **hook**. The chorus usually returns several times and is normally the catchiest part of the song. The words, melody and chord progressions of each chorus are usually identical.
Bridge	A contrasting passage between two sections of a song, sometimes referred to as a 'middle-eight' if it is eight bars long.
Instrumental	A solo section, often improvised, usually based on the chords of the verse or the chorus.
Outro or coda	A concluding section.

- **Riff**: short, repeated melodic pattern, often forming the background to a solo or vocal line; usually between one and four bars in length
- **Hook**: short, catchy melodic idea, designed to be instantly memorable
- **Guitar licks**: short solo phrases that can be heard at the ends of some vocal phrases
- **Fills**: short flourishes used to fill a gap between phrases, often played on drums.

Test yourself on Britpop

1. What is meant by Britpop?
2. What was distinctive about the music of the Beatles in the 1960s?
3. What was meant by the Manchester sound? Name two bands associated with it.
4. What helps to give Oasis their unique sound?
5. Describe three ways in which you think Oasis were influenced by the Beatles.
6. What is the difference between a verse and a chorus?

Music vocabulary test

Explain what is meant by each of the following terms:
- Hook
- Riff
- Middle-eight
- Outro.

Area of Study 4
Indian Raga, African Music and Fusions

INDIAN RAGA

There are many different styles of music in India. The music you will hear in your exam is north-Indian classical music. Most Indian classical music is based on a combination of rag, tal and drone.

What is a rag?

A rag (plural, raga) is a pattern of notes in Indian music that functions a bit like a scale or key in western music and that also forms the melodic basis of an entire piece. Each rag:

◆ Has a particular ascending and descending pattern

◆ Is associated with a different time of day, season, mood or special occasion.

What is a tal?

The tal (plural, tala) is:

◆ A repeating rhythm pattern

◆ Usually played by the tabla (small drums)

◆ Usually up to16 beats long.

The beats are grouped into small sections within the pattern. The first beat of the pattern is known as **sam**. It marks the beginnings and ends of improvisations so it is often accented.

Tintal is the most common tal. It has 16 beats (4 + 4 + 4 + 4).

It is common to mark tala by hand claps. In tintal the start of the first, second and fourth sections is marked by a clap but the beginning of the third section is weaker and this is shown by a wave of the hand, as shown in the following table.

1 2 3 4	5 6 7 8	9 10 11 12	13 14 15 16
clap	clap	wave	clap

You can hear tintal in *Rag Durga* [GAM page 122 CD3 track 13] and *Rag Brindabani Sarang* [GAM page 123 CD3 track 14].

What is a drone?

A drone is a note held (or repeated) throughout a passage of music.

Instruments

North Indian classical music groups (or ensembles) have only a handful of players. Most instruments are played while seated on the floor. The group will usually have the same three elements:

* **Soloist**: either a singer or an instrumentalist performing the melody
* **Percussion**: usually tabla
* **Drone**: either a harmonium or a tanpura.

Solo instruments

The **sitar**:

* Is a long-necked plucked string instrument with frets and a gourd resonator
* Has six or seven main strings and 12 or more sympathetic strings running underneath them
* Is played by plucking the strings with a metal plectrum
* Has a characteristic shimmering sound.

The most famous sitar player is Ravi Shankar. You can hear him playing in *Dhun in Devgiri Bilaval* [NGAM page 102 CD2 track 9].

The **sarod**:

* Is a plucked string instrument
* Is shorter than the sitar and has no frets
* Is played by plucking the strings with a large wooden plectrum
* Has main strings and sympathetic strings
* Plays ornaments by sliding up and down the strings.

Listen out for the sliding effects – these will distinguish it from a sitar.

Percussion instruments

Tabla are a pair of small drums. Their main role is to keep the time, but they also interact with the soloist and sometimes have short solos. The heads are made out of goat skin with a central area which has a coating made from iron filings and rice flour.

The smaller drum is known as the **dayan**. It is:

* Made out of wood
* Played with the fingertips of the right hand.

The larger drum is known as the **bayan**. It is:

* Made out of metal
* Played with the left hand.

Tabla playing is very difficult and students can spend years learning to master the different strokes (bols). Some strokes are open (allowed to ring) and others are closed (dampened) [NGAM page 104 CD2 track 10].

Drone instruments

The **harmonium** is a reed organ operated by bellows that open out at the back. The keyboard is on top and has a range of two or three octaves.

The **tanpura** is similar to the sitar but it has fewer strings, and unlike the sitar, plays very simple and repetitive music.

Improvisation

North Indian classical music is built on melodies which are varied by improvisation. The length of pieces is often not worked out beforehand. Some concerts are very long and all night concerts are popular in India.

A typical rag performance follows the same form. It will start out in a calm mood gradually getting more exciting throughout as the tempo and rhythmic complexity increase. The different sections are the alap, the jor and the jhalla.

The **alap**:
* Is a slow introductory section which helps to set the mood
* Has a free rhythm with no regular beat
* Is unaccompanied apart from the drone
* Usually moves from the lower notes to the higher notes
* Gradually gets faster.

The **jor**:
* Is another improvised section
* Is in a moderate tempo
* Is unaccompanied apart from the drone
* Introduces a regular pulse but there is still no metre
* Gradually gets faster.

The **jhalla**:
* Is the final section
* Has the tabla playing the tal
* Begins with a memorised composition called a gat
* Steadily gets faster until a climax is reached (at this point the gat may be repeated to end the performance).

The sections always follow the same order but some may be left out.

Learning to play raga

Indian musicians do not learn to play raga from books but by imitating and memorising. Musical information is passed on by word of mouth — this is an example of an **oral tradition**.

Students often belong to an extended family of musicians learning from a particular master. This is known as the **master-student tradition**.

Test yourself on Indian music

1. How do Indian classical musicians learn to play their instruments?
2. Describe a sitar and the way that it is played.
3. How does a sitar differ from a sarod?
4. How are tabla played?
5. What is meant by tintal?
6. North Indian classical music usually features three elements: a soloist; a percussionist; and a drone. Name three instruments that could be used to form such an ensemble.
7. A typical rag performance follows the same formal structure. Name two of the sections used and describe them.

Musical vocabulary test

Explain what is meant by each of the following:
* Rag
* Tal
* Drone
* Improvisation
* Alap
* Jor
* Jhala
* Oral tradition.

AFRICAN MUSIC

Africa is a huge continent with a wide variety of cultures and musical styles. The music you hear in your exam will be traditional music from sub-Saharan Africa – that is, south of the Sahara desert.

Here music is a big part of traditional life, from rituals to entertainment. Often everyone joins in singing, clapping or dancing, or just moving to the music.

African music:

◆ Is part of day-to-day activities as well as rites and ceremonies

◆ Has a special place in royal courts, where it also acts as a symbol of power

◆ Is not normally written down but passed on as an **oral tradition**.

Some music is performed by specialist musicians – such as **master drummers** and court musicians.

African instruments

African music is performed by a small number of instruments that have many different names.

Drums

African drums come in many shapes and sizes, from simple instruments made out of tins and oil drums to specially crafted and decorated works of art. Drums can be made from wood, metal, earthenware or large gourds. Sometimes seeds and beads are placed in the drum or rattling metal and jingles are attached to the outside.

There are many different shapes and sizes of drums:

◆ Tubular drums

◆ Bowl-shaped drums

◆ Goblet-shaped drums

◆ Friction drums

◆ Drums with two heads

◆ Drums with one head

◆ Drums small enough to be held in one hand and played with the other

◆ Drums that can be held under the armpit or with a sling

◆ Drums so large and heavy they are put on the ground to be played.

Key facts about how drums work:

1. The bigger the drum, the lower the pitch of the note.

2. The more tension in the drum head, the higher the note produced (some drums have tension strings which can be used to change the pitch of the drum).

There are many different drum-playing styles: some are played with the hands; some are played with sticks; and some are played by a combination of both hands and sticks.

In Britain, the best-known African drum is probably the west-African **djembe** (pronounced zhem-bay). It is:

* Carved from a hollowed trunk
* Covered with goat skin
* Shaped like a large goblet
* Played with the bare hands.

Talking drums is the name given to a style of drum playing that imitates the rhythms and intonations of speech. The drums can be used as signals to make announcements or warnings or to imitate speech patterns. On *Ashanti Ntumpani*, Mustapha Tettey Addy plays the atumpan – the principal talking drum of Ghana [NGAM page 106 CD2 track 11].

The music played by drum ensembles is rhythmically complex and often features **cross rhythms**. These occur when two conflicting rhythms are heard at the same time – a simple example would be triplet quavers played on one drum against straight quavers played on another. Passages based on cross rhythms are said to form a **polyrhythmic** texture.

You can see and hear examples of complex rhythms in *Nzekele* [GAM page 126 CD3 track 16].

West African drumming often uses a **time line**, a short repeated rhythm which is either clapped or played by a single or double bell, for example the **agogo** bell. The performers follow the time line which effectively holds the piece together.

The **master drummer** has the most elaborate part and plays solos. He will have had extensive training and will know a huge repertoire of rhythms. His role is to lead the drum ensemble. He does this by giving musical cues in the form of rhythm patterns. These might tell the other drummers to:

* Go to a different section
* Change drum patterns
* Change the tempo
* End the piece.

He also gives cues to dancers to signal, for example, changes of steps or tempo. You can hear a master drummer clearly in *Kundum* [GAM page 124 CD3 track 15].

String instruments

African string instruments include various types of lute, harp and zither. One is the **kora**, a long-necked African harp. The traditional role of the kora is to accompany praise songs, an important type of African music. Kora players may show off their technique by playing complicated, melodic music at dazzling speed. The Malian musician Toumani Diabete is a noted living exponent of the kora [NGAM page 111 CD2 track 12].

Other instruments

Wind instruments include flutes, horns and trumpets, and reed pipes. Flutes are often made out of bamboo.

Other instruments include rattles, shakers, gongs and rasps. Two common melodic instruments are the **mbira** (thumb piano) and the xylophone (or **balafon**). Balafons have bars made from logs or bamboo and come both with and without gourd resonators. The mbira is hand held and comes in different sizes. The thumbs play a series of wooden or metal tongues.

Singing and songs

Singing is fully integrated into daily life. There are songs for:

* Settling children, lullabies
* Counting
* Play and games
* Birthdays
* Marriages
* Work
* Drinking
* Funerals
* Religion
* Politics
* Tribal histories.

Many African languages are tonal: the pitch of the speaking voice helps to determine the meaning of the words and there is a marked difference between long and short syllables. These are the types of sound imitated by 'talking drums'.Ordinary speech tends to be melodious and performers move easily between singing and speaking.

Songs include accompanied and unaccompanied solos, duets and choruses. They are usually either split into verses or are in **call-and-response** form. In call-and-response form the leader sings a line (the call) and is answered by a chorus (the response). The chorus usually remains the same and the solo is improvised. Often there is overlapping between the lead singer and the chorus.

Melodies are usually organised within a scale of four to seven notes. They tend to be stepwise or in small intervals and often use recurring patterns and descending phrases.

African singing often includes glissandos (slides) and slurs, whistles, yodels and swoops, and types of sound that have a raspy or buzzy quality [NGAM page 111 CD2 track 13].

African music and pop music

African slaves took their music to America, where they heard the folk music of the white European settlers. From this mix came new styles of music, notably blues, gospel and jazz. These styles went on to form the basis of pop music today.

Test yourself on African music

1. Describe some of the ways in which music plays a part in African traditional life.
2. Describe the role of a master drummer.
3. What are talking drums and when might they be used?
4. Describe two ways in which different sounds can be achieved on the drums.
5. What is the function of a time line in African drumming?
6. Describe some of the rhythmic features commonly found in African music.
7. Name an African stringed instrument.
8. Describe some of the characteristics of African singing.

Music vocabulary test

Explain what is meant by each of the following:
* Balafon
* Oral tradition
* Polyrhythm
* Call-and-response
* Djembe
* Glissando.

FUSIONS

In this part of the exam you will hear music which fuses (blends) elements from either Indian or African music with features of music from another culture – often western pop music. If there is an Indian fusion there will always be a sitar and tabla among any other instruments to act as a clue.

Globalisation

During the 20th century new transport and communication systems opened up the world through television and radio, CDs and tapes, and the internet. As a result most of the world has been exposed to western pop music. This means that:

* New pop styles are springing up all over the world
* Non-western traditions have been copied by pop
* Traditional music is in danger of disappearing.

African pop music

Highlife

Highlife is one of the most well-known pop styles found in Africa. It combines African percussion instruments and western jazz instruments (such as saxophones, trumpets, vibraphones and guitars). Highlife songs are often based on west-African traditional songs, and usually have simple chords and four beats in a bar. The music has guitars, loud brass and prominent percussion, and often includes elements of:

- African rhythm
- Call and response
- Big band instrumentation
- Jazz and pop styles
- Caribbean calypso music.

Other pop styles and artists

Other African pop styles and artists include:

- **Afrobeat** (Nigeria): a fusion of highlife, soul and funk, for example by Fela Kuti
- **Juju** (Nigeria): lots of guitars and percussion, for example King Sunny Ade
- **Hiplife** (Ghana): a form of rap
- **Mbalax**: combines Cuban and Senegalese styles, for example Youssou N'Dour
- **Rap**: rap in African languages, the words deal with social injustice and political problems; political songs are common in African pop music
- **Mory Kante**: made a name for himself by combining the sound of the kora with US hip-hop and dance music
- **Salif Keita**: sometimes known as the Golden Voice of Mali, the music combines electric instruments and Cuban rhythms.

Indian fusions

When George Harrison played sitar on the Beatles' single *Norwegian Wood* in 1965 he introduced the sound of the sitar to millions of people. The Indian influence spread through pop music. During the 1970s the guitarist John McLaughlin teamed up with the Indian violinist L. Shankar and the virtuoso tabla player Zakir Hussain to combine jazz rock with Indian music in his group Shakti.

Bollywood

Bollywood is the name given to the Mumbai film industry. It comes from combining the words 'Hollywood' and 'Bombay' (the name of city now officially called Mumbai). Film music is called 'filmi'. The actors mime songs, lip-sinking over pre-recorded tracks made by professional singers. Playback singers are often stars in their own right and have their own fan base. Lata Mangeshkar is one of the most famous playback singers; she is in *The Guinness Book of Records* as the most recorded voice in the world.

Bollywood music combines elements of Indian music with elements of Western pop. The **Indian influence** can be heard in the use of:

* Traditional Indian instruments (often tabla)
* Melodies that are sometimes based on raga
* Melismatic melodies where several notes are sung to the same syllable
* Nasal vocal tone
* Vocal lines using 'gamak' – a type of gliding where notes are approached from the note above or below.

The **influence of western pop music** can be heard in the use of:

* Western instruments such as violins, synthesisers, electric guitars, clarinets, saxophone and piano
* Major or minor keys or modes
* Harmonies using simple chord patterns
* Dance rhythms: disco, foxtrot and polka rhythms are all frequently used.

You can hear these in 'Tujhe dekha to', a song taken from the Indian blockbuster movie *Dilwale Dulhania Le Jayenge* [NGAM page 129 CD2 track 16].

Bhangra

Bhangra originated in the Punjab region of India. Traditionally the people would celebrate a good harvest by dancing and singing songs to the sound of the **dhol**, a traditional north-Indian drum made from a large wooden shell and played with cane sticks. It has goat-hide skins on both sides and creates a loud sound [GAM page 136 CD3 track 18].

Bhangra is now used to describe a style of pop music developed by young British Asians and performed at Indian weddings, parties and clubs. It is a high-energy dance style of music which combines elements of western pop music, Hindi film music and folk music from the Punjabi region.

Some Classical composers have been influenced by African and Indian music, for example the minimalist composer Steve Reich who studied African drumming in Ghana.

Test yourself on fusions

1. What effect has globalisation had on the traditional music of Africa and India?

2. During the 20th century there was a big increase in the popularity of fusion styles in music. Give four reasons for this.

3. Name some of the pop music styles to be found in Africa.

4. Describe Highlife music.

5. What were the origins of UK bhangra dance music?

6. When would you normally hear (a) traditional bhangra (b) western pop bhangra played?

7. Bollywood music combines elements of Indian music with elements of western pop music. Name two Indian influences and two influences from western pop music.

8. What is a dhol drum?

Listening practice

The questions below are designed to provide useful practice in listening. They can be applied to most pieces, although not every question can be applied to every piece. You will find some useful tips on the types of answers required at the end of this section.

♦ How many beats are there in each bar?

♦ Give an example of syncopation.

♦ What is the rhythm of the bass line?

Sometimes you will be asked to name an interval or to write out few notes from a piece. You can practise this by trying to identify intervals or to write out parts of the main themes.

♦ What is the range of the melody?

♦ Is the opening phrase legato or staccato?

♦ Is this piece in a major or a minor key?

♦ Describe the chord sequence.

♦ What type of cadence does the piece end with?

♦ What is a likely metronome marking for this piece?

♦ What is a likely bpm (beats per minute) for this piece?

♦ Use an Italian term to describe the tempo of this piece.

♦ What form is the piece in?

♦ What are the main features of this form?

♦ What is the structure of the verse? (for example, AABA)

♦ How does the middle-eight differ from the verse in this song?

♦ Describe the hook.

♦ Describe the riff.

♦ Describe the introduction (or intro).

♦ Describe the outro (or coda).

♦ Describe the dynamics.

♦ Where does the climax come in the piece?

♦ Give an example of a crescendo.

♦ Give an example of a diminuendo.

♦ Give an example of dynamic contrast.

♦ In which decade do you think that this song was recorded?

♦ Identify three ways in which music technology is used.

♦ Give an example of a sample in this song.

♦ Give an example of a loop in this song.

♦ Describe the electronic the effects used in this song.

♦ How would you describe the texture of this music?

◆ Is the texture homophonic, monophonic or polyphonic?

◆ Name the instruments playing.

◆ Name the solo instrument(s) heard.

◆ Name the instrument (or instruments) playing the bass line.

◆ Which family of instruments does this (or these) instrument(s) belong to?

◆ Name the playing techniques used.

◆ What is the name of this style of music? Give reasons for your answer.

◆ What are the main musical characteristics of this style?

◆ When was this piece composed?

◆ What decade does this song come from? Give reasons for your answer.

◆ Describe the mood of this music. How do the musical elements combine to create this mood?

◆ How does the music reflect the words?

Useful tips

Always try to be specific in your answers. For example, if you are asked to name the type of ensemble playing, identify it as a string quartet or string orchestra rather than just 'strings'.

If you are asked to describe the vocal melody, try to include locations, such as 'low and moving in step at the start, then wider leaps follow leading to a high register at the end'.

Rhythm

Most music has either two, three or four beats in a bar. These are sometimes referred to as duple, triple and quadruple metre. Most pop songs have four beats in a bar. The most common time signature is $\frac{4}{4}$ (logically also known as **common time**). This means that there are four crotchet beats in a bar.

To work out how many beats there are in a bar, listen out for the strong beats (which come at the beginning of each bar) and then count how many beats there are in each bar.

Syncopation is where off-beats are accented. It is found a great deal in pop music.

When you are describing a rhythm you do not always have to talk about note lengths. You can also talk about them in terms of repeated rhythms, syncopated rhythms, dotted rhythms, long notes, short notes and so on. Some rhythms are repetitive and predictable – these could be described as regular rhythms.

Melody

An **interval** is the distance between two notes. Two notes next to each other (for example C and D) are a second apart, two notes with a note in between (for example C and E) are a third apart and so on.

Many melodies use a lot of stepwise movement and small intervals – others might include wider intervals (leaps).

Many melodies consist of two or more phrases, often of equal lengths.

Many musical terms are in Italian. The term **legato** is Italian for smooth whereas **staccato** means detached. The **range of a melody** refers to the distance between the highest and the lowest notes of the tune. The **tessitura** is the part of the pitch range (for example high or low) in which a passage of music mainly lies.

Harmony and tonality

Many pieces are in a major or minor key throughout. This is known as **diatonic** harmony. When a piece changes key it is said to have **modulated**. Sometimes a piece will start in a minor key and end in a major key.

Many phrases will end with **cadences**. There are four types of cadences: perfect, imperfect, plagal, interrupted – learn to recognise the sound of these.

Many pop songs have repeated chord patterns. It is useful to mention that there is a repeated chord pattern even if you cannot pinpoint what the chords are. If a piece has a clear sense of being in one or more keys, it is said to be **tonal**. If it has no sense of key it is said to be **atonal** – most atonal music includes frequent and often harsh discords.

Tempo

The tempo of a song is the speed of the underlying beat. It can be described by Italian terms such as **largo** (very slow), **adagio** (slow), **andante** (walking pace), **moderato** (moderate speed), **vivace** (lively), **allegro** (quick) or **presto** (very fast).

Tempo can also be worked out in bpm or beats per minute. You can usually work the bpm out approximately by looking at the second hand on your watch. This will give you 60bpm. A beat that is twice as fast will be 120bpm and so on.

A **metronome marking** tells you how many beats there are per minute and also tells you the type of beat, for example 60 crotchets per minute.

Sometimes the tempo is very strict and stays the same throughout a piece of music, at other times it will be more free. This is sometimes known as **rubato**. When a piece of music gets gradually faster this is known as an **accelerando**. When it gets gradually slower this is known as a **ritardando** or **rallentando**.

Form or structure

The form of a piece is usually based on repetition and contrast. Listen out for the different sections. These can be analysed using letter names (A, B, C) where a new letter name identifies a new feature or section.

Some structural devices are easy to recognise such as **ground bass**, **rondo**, and **variations**. Within the overall form of the music, there will usually be other structural devices such as **riffs**, **ostinati** (where a rhythmic, melodic or harmonic pattern is repeated) and **motifs** (short melodic or rhythmic ideas which are manipulated and modified).

The majority of pop songs are in **verse-and-chorus** form. The structure of the verse can be analysed using letter names where a new letter name identifies a new section, usually a different melody and chord pattern. There may be a **middle-eight**, a contrasting section which is usually differentiated by having either a different melody, chord pattern or by being played by different instruments. The words may also have a different subject.

Listen out for riffs and hooks. A **riff** is a short, repeated melodic pattern, often forming the background to a solo or vocal line, or to a whole song. It is usually up to four bars long. A hook is a short catchy melodic idea designed to be instantly memorable.

Intros of pop sings often consist of one of the following:

◆ An instrumental version of the verse
◆ A short chord pattern leading to the opening of the song
◆ A build up of layers of instruments.

An **outro** or **coda** brings the song to a close. Outros often consist of one of the following:

◆ An instrumental version of the verse or chorus
◆ A reduction in the layers of instruments
◆ Loud and definite or quiet and questioning music
◆ A repeat of the last few bars of the song that gradually fade out.

Dance music is usually a collage of samples and loops. The main sections of dance music can usually be identified as mix in, the main section, breakdown and mix out.

Dynamics

Dynamics are varying degrees of loud and quiet. The dynamics can be described using Italian terms such as **forte** (loud), **mezzo forte** (moderately loud), **piano** (quiet) or **pianissimo** (very quiet). Sometimes the dynamics are contrasted with whole sections being loud or quiet. At other times the music may get gradually louder or quieter. When the music gradually gets louder this is known a **crescendo**. When the music gradually gets quieter, this is known as a **diminuendo**.

Music technology

Music technology will usually be found in the use of **electronic instruments** (for example synthesiser, drum machine), **recording techniques** (sequences, samples and loops), **recording effects** (phasing, panning, echo, reverb and so on). Try not to confuse effects with instruments or techniques.

Instrumentation

The word **instrumentation** refers to the instruments and voices heard and they way they are used. When you are asked to name an **instrumental family** remember to name the family and not the instrument. Remember that there are four families of orchestral instruments: **strings, woodwind, brass** and **percussion**.

Sometimes you will be asked to say whether a voice is **soprano, alto, tenor** or **bass**. If you hear a woman's voice then the answer is either soprano or alto (or contralto, they mean the same thing). If you hear a man's voice then the answer is tenor or bass. If you hear a child's voice the answer is treble. Occasionally you will hear a man singing in a high register; in this case the answer is **falsetto**, sometimes referred to as **countertenor** (or male alto). The large majority of music for this voice range was written during the Baroque period, so that should help you with the rest of the question. **A cappella** refers to unaccompanied singing.

Texture

The **texture** of a piece of music refers to the overall picture of the sound. It can be described in terms of how many layers there are, whether the music is dense or sparse, whether it uses mainly chords or single notes and so on. The word **monophonic** is used to describe a texture which has a single unaccompanied melody, whereas a **homophonic** texture is one in which a single part has the melody and the other parts provide a simple accompaniment. A **polyphonic** (or **contrapuntal**) texture has two or more melodies sounding together.

Timbre

The word **timbre** can be used to describe the instrumental colour, the quality that makes one sound (like a flute) different from another (such as a trumpet). Instruments can also produce different sounds through a range of playing techniques. You should be clear what is meant by **playing techniques**. These are the different ways that an instrument can be played. Think of your own instrument – if it is a guitar then you will be familiar with plucking, strumming and picking. A string player, may pluck the strings (**pizzicato**) or bow the strings (**arco**).

Style

To describe the main musical characteristics of any style (for example minimalism or house music) think of the instruments, rhythms, playing techniques, forms, harmony and so on, typically used. Be sure to take account of all the evidence you hear and don't just rely on one feature. The mood of a song is usually easily determined from the lyrics and reflected in the music. A sad song is quite likely to be slow and quiet; it may feature falling phrases and could well be in a minor key. But don't assume it will necessarily have all of these features.

Sample questions

The sample questions that follow are the type that you will get in your exam. You will find recordings of all these pieces in *The New GCSE Anthology of Music* (ed) Julia Winterson (Peters Edition Ltd 2000).

AREA OF STUDY 1

Structure in western classical music 1600–1899

Listen to the following extract from Pachelbel's *Canon* which will be played **four** times.

1. What is the tonality of the extract? Underline your answer.

   atonal   major   minor   modal

2. Choose one word from the following list to describe the texture. Underline your answer.

   monophonic   homophonic   polyrhythmic   polyphonic

3. Which string instrument plays the ground bass?

   ....

4. Complete the pitch of the bass line. The rhythm is given above the stave.

5. The bass line uses a sequence. What is a sequence?

   ....

   ....

6. This piece uses canon. Explain what is meant by canon. You should make **three** points in your answer.

   ....

   ....

   ....

AREA OF STUDY 2

Changing directions in western classical music from 1900

Listen **four** times to this extract from *Zoom Tube* by Ian Clarke.

1. Which word best describes the style of this piece. Underline your answer.

   experimental   electronic   expressionism   serialism

2. Name the instrument playing.

   ....

3. Which orchestral family does this instrument belong to?

   ....

4. Describe the dynamics in the opening bars. You should make **four** points in your answer.

   ....

   ....

   ....

   ....

5. This piece uses extended instrumental techniques. What are extended instrumental techniques?

   ....

   ....

6. Give **two** examples of extended instrumental techniques that you can hear in this piece.

   ....

   ....

AREA OF STUDY 3

Popular music in context

Listen **four** times to the opening of *The Boxer* by the Chemical Brothers.

1. How many beats are there in a bar? Underline your answer.

    2   3   4   5

2. What is the approximate bpm of this song? Underline your answer.

    60 bpm   97 bpm   132bpm   240 bpm

3. Which of the following best describes the three piano chords used. Underline your answer.
    (a) They are all major chords
    (b) They are all minor chords
    (c) The first two chords are major and the third chord is minor
    (d) The first chord is major and the second and third chords are minor.

4. Give **two** ways in which the piano chords have been treated using technology.

    ....

    ....

5. The song has a breakdown section using a cappella vocals. What is meant by:

    a) Breakdown ....

    ....

    b) A cappella ....

    ....

6. A drum loop is used. What is a loop?

    ....

    ....

AREA OF STUDY 4

Indian raga, African music and fusions

Listen **three** times to the first two verses of 'Tujhe dekha to'.

1. What is the interval between the first two notes of the song?

   ....

2. Choose **three** words from the following list which could be used to describe the introduction. Underline your answers.

largo	vivace	ornamented	figured bass
rubato	polyrhythm	col legno	staccato

3. Which of the following best describes the string parts used. Underline your answer.
   a) They play an ascending line in unison
   b) They play a descending line in octaves
   c) They play an ascending line in thirds.

4. Name a percussion instrument that you can hear.

   ....

5. Give **two** characteristics of Indian music and two characteristics of western music that you can hear.

   ....

   ....

   ....

   ....

Sample answers

Structure in western classical music 1600–1899

1. Major
2. Polyphonic
3. Cello
4.

5. The immediate repetition of phrase or motif in the same part at a different pitch from the original.
6. Any **three** of:
   - The melody in one part is imitated throughout in another part while the melody in the first part continues
   - There may be several such imitative parts
   - Each part follows the previous one exactly (note-for-note) although it may be at a higher or lower pitch
   - A canon is a type of counterpoint.

Changing directions in western classical music from 1900

1. Experimental
2. Flute
3. Woodwind
4. All of:
   - Starts off very quietly / *pp* / pianissimo
   - Followed by a crescendo
   - Very loud / *ff*
   - Then a diminuendo to nothing.
5. Unusual sounds created by playing an instrument in an unconventional way.
6. Any **two** of:
   - Multiphonics
   - Quarter tones
   - Singing into instrument
   - Note bending
   - Breathy tone.

AREA OF STUDY 3

Popular music in context

1. 4
2. 97 bpm
3. d) The first chord is major and the second and third chords are minor.
4. Both of:
   * Sampled
   * Sequenced.
5. a) Breakdown – the sounds drop out in order to create tension when they build up again.
   b) A cappella – unaccompanied singing.
6. Where a short section of recorded sound is repeated over and over again.

AREA OF STUDY 4

Indian raga, African music and fusions

1. A 5th
2. All of:
   * Largo
   * Ornamented
   * Rubato.
3. a) They play an ascending line in unison.
4. Tambourine or tabla
5. Indian:
   * Indian instruments, for example tabla / santoor
   * Nasal timbre of vocal line
   * Ornaments in vocal line (gamak).
   Western:
   * Western instruments, for example strings
   * Western harmony
   * Major and minor chords
   * Simple chord pattern.